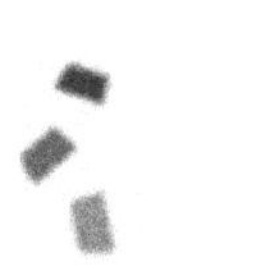

Novels for Students, Volume 35

Project Editor: Sara Constantakis Rights Acquisition and Management: Margaret Chamberlain-Gaston, Leitha Etheridge-Sims, Kelly Quin, Aja Perales Composition: Evi Abou-El-Seoud Manufacturing: Drew Kalasky

Imaging: John Watkins

Product Design: Pamela A. E. Galbreath, Jennifer Wahi Content Conversion: Katrina Coach Product Manager: Meggin Condino

For product information and technology assistance, contact us at **Gale Customer Support, 1-800-877-4253.**
For permission to use material from this text or product, submit all requests online at www.cengage.com/permissions.
Further permissions questions can be emailed to **permissionrequest@cengage.com** While every effort has been made to ensure the reliability of the information presented in this publication, Gale, a part of Cengage Learning, does not guarantee the accuracy of the data contained herein. Gale accepts no payment for listing; and inclusion in the publication of any organization, agency, institution, publication, service, or individual does not imply endorsement of the editors or publisher. Errors brought to the attention of the publisher and verified to the satisfaction of the publisher will be corrected in future editions.

Gale
27500 Drake Rd.
Farmington Hills, MI, 48331-3535

ISBN-13: 978-1-4144-6698-9
ISBN-10: 1-4144-6698-6
ISSN 1094-3552

This title is also available as an e-book.
ISBN-13: 978-1-4144-7364-2

ISBN-10: 1-4144-7364-8
Contact your Gale, a part of Cengage Learning sales representative for ordering information.

Printed in the United States of America
1 2 3 4 5 6 7 14 13 12 11 10

Maus: A Survivor's Tale

Art Spiegelman 1986–1991

Introduction

Art Spiegelman's *Maus: A Survivor's Tale* is a two-volume graphic novel that documents the survival of the author's parents, both Polish Jews, during the Holocaust. Spiegelman depicts Jews as mice—hence the title—and Germans as cats as a metaphor for how Jews were hunted and killed in accordance with the Nazi Party's planned extermination of all European Jews during World War II. Spiegelman began work on the story as early as 1971, and he published portions of the story between 1980 and 1986 in the underground graphic journal *RAW*, which he edited with his wife, Françoise Mouly.

The first volume of *Maus*, subtitled *My Father Bleeds History*, was published to critical acclaim in 1986; the second volume, *And Here My Troubles Began*, followed in 1991. *Maus* is as much a story about how the author's parents, Vladek and Anja Spiegelman, narrowly escaped death in Auschwitz as it is about their son's struggle to translate their personal history into a meaningful narrative and come to terms with the effect it has had on his own life.

Maus broke new ground in the graphic novel genre. Both volumes were nominated for the National Book Critics Circle Award, and in 1992 the work received a Pulitzer Prize in the Special Awards and Citations—Letters category. It also received the two highest honors in the field of graphic novels, the Eisner Award for Best Graphic Album and the Harvey Award for Best Graphic Album of Previously Published Work. *Maus* was arguably the first graphic novel to reach a mass audience, and it paved the way for other serious works in the genre. As a work of Holocaust literature, it has garnered praise and critical analysis on par with landmark works of the genre, including Elie Wiesel's *Night* and Primo Levi's *Survival in Auschwitz*.

Author Biography

Spiegelman was born on February 15, 1948, in Stockholm, Sweden, to Vladek and Anja Spiegelman, Polish Jews and Holocaust survivors who immigrated to the country after World War II. When Art was three, the family moved to Rego Park, a neighborhood in Queens, New York. Spiegelman was captivated by *Mad* magazine and Golden Age comic books as a child and attended the High School of Art and Design in Manhattan. While at Harpur College, he began working for the Topps Chewing Gum Corporation, where he created Wacky Packages and Garbage Pail Kids trading cards over the course of a twenty-year association with the company. When Spiegelman was twenty, he suffered a nervous breakdown and spent time in a mental hospital. Shortly afterward, his mother, who had suffered from depression for many years, committed suicide.

Spiegelman was a key figure in the alternative comics—or "comix" as they were affectionately known—movement of the late 1960s and early 1970s in San Francisco. During this time he published "Prisoner on the Hell Planet," an account of his mother's suicide that was later reprinted in *Maus* and that was also collected in 1977's *Breakdowns: From Maus to Now: An Anthology of Strips*. Spiegelman returned to New York in 1976 and married Francçoise Mouly, a former architecture student from France. In 1980, they founded the alternative comics journal *RAW*, where portions of *Maus* first appeared. The publication of the first volume of *Maus* in 1986 thrust him into the spotlight as a major writer and leading graphic novelist. The second volume, published in 1991, garnered him a Pulitzer Prize and solidified his position as a major figure in Holocaust literature.

From 1991 to 2003, Spiegelman was a staff artist at *The New Yorker*. He contributed many covers to the magazine, the most famous of which is his September 24, 2001, black-on-black illustration featuring the barely visible silhouette of the World Trade Center twin towers. The image later became the cover of his book *In the Shadow of No Towers*, his graphic novel about the 9/11 attacks near his home in lower Manhattan. Though the anthologized panels that comprise the 2004 book were controversial because of Spiegelman's visceral reactions to terrorism and the wars that followed, critics praised the volume, and *Time* magazine listed Spiegelman as one of their Top 100 Most Influential People in 2005.

As an advocate for the graphic novel and comics in general, Spiegelman lectures frequently and has taught at the University of California at Santa Cruz and the School of Visual Arts in New York. Spiegelman and Mouly have worked together on a number of projects, including the “Little Lit” series, an anthology of comics for children by such authors as Lemony Snicket, Maurice Sendak, William Joyce, and Neil Gaiman.

Plot Summary

Volume I: My Father Bleeds History

The book opens in the mid-1970s with the adult Art, who is drawn as a mouse with a human body, visiting his father, Vladek, and his second wife, Mala, for dinner at their home in Rego Park, Queens. Art and his father are not close, and the tension between them is instantly apparent. Vladek and Mala have a tumultuous marriage—she complains that he is a miser, and he complains that she is a spendthrift. After dinner, Art asks his dad to recount his life before and during World War II in hopes of turning it into a graphic novel. Vladek reluctantly agrees.

Vladek's story is seen in flashbacks as he narrates it to Art. Vladek starts in the 1930s, when he was selling textiles in Czestochowa, Poland, near the German border. Through a cousin who lives in Sosnowiec, he meets Anja Zylberberg, a nice but nervous girl from a wealthy family. They are married in 1937, and Vladek begins working for his father-in-law.

On Art's next visit to Rego Park his father throws out his long winter trench coat and replaces it with a short jacket. When Art discovers this, he is enraged. Vladek, who has one glass eye, cataracts in the other, and is diabetic, busies himself counting pills. Between these domestic events, Vladek continues his story. Early in his marriage, he catches Anja translating documents for the Communists. The police search their apartment, but Anja has left the documents with a neighbor who is arrested instead. Vladek orders Anja to cease all such sordid activity and she does.

Vladek becomes the supervisor of a textile factory in Bielsko, and Anja has a baby boy named Richieu. Anja suffers from postpartum depression, so she and Vladek travel to a luxurious sanitarium in Czechoslovakia. On the way they see their first Nazi swastika flag; it is 1938, and stories of violent pogroms against Jews are becoming increasingly common.

Vladek is drafted into the Polish army on the eve of World War II. In one of the war's first battles, Vladek kills a German soldier and is taken prisoner. One night he has a dream about Parshas Truma, an annual day on the Jewish calendar. An imprisoned rabbi tells him this is auspicious, and sure enough, three months later he is released from the prisoner of war (POW) camp on Parshas Truma. Instead of returning to Sosnowiec, he ends up at another POW camp in Lublin. He obtains his release by calling upon the assistance of some family friends in the town and sneaks back to Sosnowiec. Amonth after his return his mother dies of cancer.

Media Adaptations

- The Voyager Company released *The Complete Maus* on CD-ROM in 1994. The multimedia disc includes the book, preliminary drawings, journal entries, home movies, and audio of some of the tape-recorded conversations between Art and Vladek Spiegelman.
- "Making Maus," an exhibition featuring Spiegelman's original artwork, ran at the Museum of Modern Art in New York City in 1991.

When Art next visits Rego Park, he brings a tape recorder, and Vladek continues his story. Twelve family members, including Vladek, Anja, and Richieu, are living with Anja's father in their well-appointed Sosnowiec apartment, but life is not safe for the Jews. Many are carried off to work camps; food is rationed. Vladek forges useful alliances that enable him to keep working and to barter for food on the black market. Vladek's in-laws make a deal to sell their furniture to some German officers, but the officers take the furniture without paying for it. Vladek wants to send Richieu to live in safety with another family, but Anja refuses.

On January 1, 1942, all Jews in Sosnowiec are forcibly moved to the ghetto. Vladek, Anja, and eleven other family members now share two small rooms. Several of the men Vladek does business with are hanged. He stops selling cloth and starts dealing in gold and jewelry, which is easier to hide. Vladek mentions that Anja kept voluminous diaries about the war, and Art desperately wants them. Vladek says he has thrown them out.

Next, the Germans decree that Jews older than seventy will be taken to a special senior community.

They hide Anja's elderly grandparents behind a false wall in a shed. Officials threaten to take Anja's father in their place, and thus the grandparents are handed over. They are immediately sent to the gas chambers at Auschwitz.

Sosnowiec's remaining Jews are forced to have their documents inspected and stamped at the town's sports stadium. Healthy, able-bodied workers are separated from the elderly, the sick, and families with many young children. Only the healthy—about ten thousand people, Vladek and Anja among them —receive stamped papers and are allowed to return to the ghetto. Everyone else is taken away and never seen again. Mala says her mother was taken from the stadium that day and housed with thousands of other Jews in a nearby apartment building until they were discovered and sent to the gas chambers at Auschwitz. Art scours the house in vain looking for his mother's diaries. Mala complains that Vladek has saved everything—except for the diaries—and that he is more attached to things than people.

During Art's next visit to Rego Park, he discovers that his father has just read a comic Art wrote years ago about his mother's suicide. Titled "Prisoner on the Hell Planet," it is reprinted on the following pages. Drawn in a scratchboard style based on German Expressionist art, it depicts Art, recently discharged from a mental hospital, wearing a striped uniform much like the one worn by concentration camp prisoners. His mother slits her wrists and dies in the bathtub. Art blames his dead mother for his feelings of despair and his father for being needy and distraught. Vladek admits the story made him cry and brought back many memories of his beloved Anja.

On a walk to the bank, Vladek resumes his story. In 1943, the remaining Sosnowiec Jews are moved to the ghetto of Srodula, where they are under lock and key. Anja and Vladek decide to send Richieu to live with Anja's sister, where they believe he will be safer, but when the Gestapo liquidates that ghetto, Anja's sister poisons herself, her children, and Richieu in order to spare them from the gas chambers at Auschwitz.

The Germans begin to liquidate the Srodula ghetto, and Vladek builds a bunker in the cellar of their small cottage. When that becomes too dangerous, they hide in the attic of a different house. Eventually they are betrayed and taken to a prison to await transport to Auschwitz. Vladek tries to spare his in-laws by bribing officials.

They take his jewels but send Anja's parents to the gas chambers at Auschwitz anyway. Vladek survives by forming a friendship with a Jewish police officer who plays cards with the Gestapo. When Vladek and Anja are the only ones left in their family, Anja becomes hysterical and wants to die. Vladek tells her that to die is easy but to stay alive is hard. Together they will keep each other strong and survive.

Art and Vladek arrive at the bank, where Vladek gives Art a key to his safe deposit box. He complains that Mala wants to steal all his money. Art tells his father to enjoy his wealth, but Vladek insists on hiding it in the bank. He still has a few gold trinkets left from the war. On another visit to Rego Park, Mala complains to Art that Vladek treats her like a servant and does not give her enough money for essentials. Mala says his stinginess has nothing to do with surviving the prison camps, because she knows plenty of survivors, none of whom are as miserly as he is. Vladek complains that Mala is greedy and obsessed with money. However, both of them are impressed with Art's initial drawings for the book.

Vladek and Anja walk back to Sosnowiec after the Srodula ghetto is liquidated. For several months they alternate between hiding in a barn outside town and staying at a house in town owned by a woman named Motonowa. They arrange to escape to Hungary, which they believe is safer than Poland, but they are betrayed en route and delivered to the gates of Auschwitz. At Auschwitz they are separated, and neither believes they will survive.

Art asks again for his mother's notebooks. Vladek says he burned them after Anja's suicide because they held too many painful memories. Art yells at his father for saving useless junk and destroying priceless memories. He storms out in anger, calling his father a murderer.

Volume II: And Here My Troubles Began

In the summer of 1979, Vladek interrupts Art and Françoise's vacation with the news that Mala has left him and taken all his money. He urges them to spend the rest of the summer at his rented cabin in the Catskills. The thought fills them with dread, but they agree to visit for a few days. Art is finding his graphic novel difficult; how can he make sense of the Holocaust if he cannot make sense of his relationship with his parents? He feels guilty for having had an easier life than his parents and remarks that he had a childhood sibling rivalry with

Richieu's portrait, which hung in his parents' bedroom.

In the Catskills, Vladek complains endlessly about Mala and asks Art and Françoise to come live with him in Rego Park. They do not want to live with him but recognize that he is in bad health and needs assistance. Vladek continues his story with his arrival at Auschwitz. Although he and Anja were quickly separated (she was sent to nearby Birkenau), he says they were always together during the war. Vladek and a wealthy former business associate, Mandelbaum, are processed and housed together. Their prisoner numbers are tattooed on their forearms. A rabbi tells Vladek that his prison number is auspicious, and this gives him hope. Mandelbaum is miserable. It is winter, and he has only one shoe, pants that are too big, no belt, and no spoon.

Vladek volunteers to teach English to the kapo (a Polish prisoner who serves as a supervisor). In return, the kapo saves him from the gas chamber and arranges for him to get a nice uniform and leather shoes. Vladek also obtains a belt, shoes, and spoon for Mandelbaum, who thanks him profusely and declares them gifts from God. Several days later Mandelbaum is taken away and never seen again.

In Chapter 2, "Auschwitz (Time Flies)," Art is at his desk working. He is wearing a mouse mask, and flies are buzzing around the room. Dead bodies are piled at his feet. He summarizes the story thus far: Vladek died in 1982, he is working on this page in 1987, and he and Françoise are expecting their first child. In 1986 the first volume of *Maus* was published, but he is uncomfortable with his success. He feels guilty; he wants everyone to feel guilty. In each succeeding frame he appears smaller until he is the size of a child, whereupon he screams for his mommy. He decides to visit his therapist, Pavel, who also survived the concentration camps. Both of them are wearing mouse masks. Art tells Pavel about his writer's block. Pavel talks about survivor's guilt and how maybe there should not be any more Holocaust stories. Art invokes a quotation from writer Samuel Beckett about silence. Walking home, Art returns to normal size and reports that he feels much better.

In Auschwitz, Vladek proves adept at forming associations with key people in order to get himself extra food and to prevent starving or being sent to the gas chamber. He is assigned to work in a tin shop after claiming he knows how to do the work. Vladek befriends Mancie, a beautiful Hungarian girl who is having a relationship with a German officer and who passes notes and food from Vladek to Anja. Mancie risks her life to foster communication between them, believing their love deserves it. In Birkenau, Anja, who has always been weak and now appears as little more than a skeleton, is forced to carry large pots of soup that are too heavy for her. She spills constantly, and the guards beat her for it.

Vladek volunteers for the work detail at Birkenau, risking his life in order to glimpse Anja. Once, Vladek is caught speaking to her and severely beaten. Back at Auschwitz, more and more prisoners are falling ill. The Germans kill all who are no longer capable of work. Vladek volunteers to become a shoemaker and quickly learns yet another new skill. He is very good at it and curries favor with some of the German officials. He receives extra food, which he barters for favors from the kapo. Anja is moved to a new barracks in Auschwitz that is closer to Vladek—it is the only time in the camp that he is happy.

Once when Vladek sneaks food to Anja, she is chased by a guard. The guard threatens to kill her, but she disappears into the barracks, and her identity is never discovered. The next day the guards urge others in the barracks to turn her in. No one does. Meanwhile, Vladek has become quite weak. He is in danger of being sent to the gas chamber, so he hides in the bathroom during one of the periodic "selection" examinations. By now the Russians are closing in. Vladek and a few others are sent to dismantle the gas chambers. He describes them in detail, and Art provides a drawing of them. A fellow prisoner tells Vladek that after each gassing, he was forced to pry apart piles of dead, mangled bodies and shovel them in to the furnaces. He also describes throwing people into pits and burning them alive.

As the Russians get closer, the Germans abandon Auschwitz and force the prisoners on a hundred-mile death march to Breslau, Germany. Those who cannot keep up are shot. Breslau is in chaos; within a few days Vladek is herded onto a cattle car with roughly two hundred other people. The train departs from Breslau but does not go far before it comes to a halt. The prisoners are locked inside with nothing to eat for about a week. Vladek survives by forming a hammock out of his blanket, which suspends him above the crush of bodies and enables him to grab snow off the roof of the train. The Germans unlock the doors only long enough for them to throw out the dead bodies. Eventually, when only a few of them are still alive, the train begins moving. At a Red Cross station they each receive a care package of food. It is February 1945.

The train takes them to Dachau, where there is nothing to do but wait to die. Vladek survives by striking up a friendship with a Frenchman who shares food with him in return for the opportunity to practice his English. He trades some of this food for a shirt with no lice. He wears the shirt only at inspection time; only prisoners with no lice can receive food.

Vladek's situation becomes bleaker when he contracts typhus. He steps on dead bodies each night to get to the bathroom. He becomes so weak he cannot get out of bed or even eat. He trades his bread to two others in exchange for help in getting to the bathroom. Eventually his fever breaks. Again, the camp is evacuated, and all able-bodied prisoners are marched to a train to be exchanged for German POWs at the Swiss border. Vladek is carried to the train by the men he paid to take him to the bathroom.

Back in the Catskills, Vladek is still

disgruntled over Mala's inconsiderate departure. He packs up her opened boxes of food and takes them back to the grocery store. He argues with the store manager, telling him he is a Holocaust survivor and receives six dollars' worth of food for only a dollar.

On the way back from the grocery store, Françoise stops to give a ride to an African American hitchhiker. Vladek becomes extremely irritated, calls the man a *shvartser*, and worries he will steal the groceries. They drop the man off without incident. Françoise and Art rebuke Vladek for his racism, but he is unrepentant. Françoise says he talks about the blacks like the Nazis talked about the Jews, but Vladek disagrees. There is no comparison between blacks and Jews, he says, and she should be smart enough to know better.

Back in Rego Park, Vladek laments that his money and his health are gone. Art asks more about Anja. She left Auschwitz earlier than Vladek and spent time in Ravensbruck, a women's concentration camp. Anja was liberated near the Russian front earlier than Vladek and returned to Sosnowiec.

Vladek's train from Dachau never reaches the Swiss border. Instead, it stops, and a rumor spreads that the war is over. German soldiers seem not to know what to do with them. They are rounded up several times, believing they will be shot but are then released again. Eventually, Vladek and a friend, Shivek, hide out in an abandoned house. The Americans arrive a few days later, and after a while Vladek and Shivek report to a displaced persons camp.

Vladek shares with Art old photos of those on Anja's side of the family, some of whom survived the war and some of whom did not. On Vladek's side of the family, only his younger brother survived. Vladek's heart starts bothering him, and he must rest. Art apologizes for making him talk so much, but Vladek says that it is always a pleasure.

Vladek goes to Florida, and Art and Françoise fret about what to do when he returns. He is too ill to live on his own, but they do not want to move to Rego Park. Mala calls from Florida; she and Vladek have reunited, but now Vladek is in the hospital. She wants them to come down and help bring him back to a hospital in New York. When they arrive, Vladek is bedridden. He continues his story: After the war he and Anja left for Sweden, where he reestablished himself in the garment industry and Art was born. Vladek wants to stay in Sweden, but Anja wants to move to New York where she has relatives.

Vladek and Mala return briefly to New York before deciding to permanently relocate to Florida. By now, Vladek is starting to have memory problems. In their final interview session, Vladek recalls how he and Shivek received new papers at the displaced persons camp and departed for Hannover to stay with Shivek's family. Vladek tries to learn Anja's whereabouts through the Jewish community center in Sosnowiec, but he fears the worst. He travels to Belsen, where many Jewish refugees are gathering, and runs into acquaintances from Sosnowiec who say Anja is alive. He makes the arduous journey home, which takes three or four weeks because of the destruction of the rail lines. Eventually they are reunited.

Vladek retreats to bed, mistaking Art for his dead son, Richieu. The final image in the book shows Vladek and Anja's headstone, adorned only with the years of their births and deaths. Art signs his name below with the dates 1971–1994—the years in which he wrote the book.

Characters

Mancie

Mancie is a prisoner in Birkenau, the death camp sometimes called Auschwitz II. She is a beautiful Hungarian girl who ferries messages and food between Vladek and Anja, which helps Anja survive. Mancie is brave—if her actions are discovered she will be killed immediately. She is also reputed to be having an affair with a Nazi officer, which accounts for her ability to move between the camps more freely than the other prisoners. She agrees to help Vladek and Anja because she believes their love deserves it. Vladek regrets that he never learned her last name and was thus unable to compensate her for helping to keep Anja alive.

Mandelbaum

Mandelbaum is one of Vladek's former business associates, a millionaire in prewar Poland who is transferred to Auschwitz in the same group as Vladek. Mandelbaum's miserable circumstances at Auschwitz provide a rare moment of comedy in the story. He has only one shoe, which keeps falling off, his pants are too big, and he has no belt. He dropped his spoon while he was trying to hold his pants up and now has no utensil to eat with. Vladek, through his association with the kapo, arranges to get Mandelbaum real leather shoes, a belt, and a spoon. For this, Mandelbaum thanks him profusely, saying they are gifts from God. Several days later Mandelbaum is taken away and never seen again.

Françoise Mouly

Level-headed and supportive, Françoise is Art's wife and artistic comrade. Art struggles with how to portray her. She wants to be a mouse because she converted to Judaism when they married. Art finally relents after considering making her a frog (because she is French) or a reindeer. Françoise helps sort out Vladek's finances after Mala abandons him in the Catskills but angers Vladek when she picks up an African American hitchhiker. She notes that his distrust of black people is reminiscent of how the Germans treated the Jews, but he rebukes her for her naivete´.

Pavel

Pavel is Art's psychotherapist, a Czechoslovakian Jew, and an Auschwitz survivor. He sees patients only at night and keeps framed pictures of his cats in his office. In his session with Art, both of the mare drawn as humans wearing mouse masks as they discuss survivor's guilt and whether or not Art should give the world yet another Holocaust story. Art says that Pavel always makes him feel better, which is illustrated by Art's growth from a child-sized representation to his normal size on his walk home from the session.

Anja Spiegelman

Anja Spiegelman is Vladek's first wife and Art's mother. She is the pivotal figure in both Vladek's and Art's stories, yet her suicide and the destruction of her diaries prevent her from telling her own story in the book. By all accounts, she is a nervous, frail woman who was on medication even before her marriage to Vladek. Following the birth of Richieu, her depression reaches clinical proportions, and Vladek takes her for a three-month stay at a ritzy sanitarium.

During the hardships of the war, Anja tells Vladek that she wants to die. Vladek makes her promise to stay alive, because dying is easy and survival is hard. She displays little of the ingenuity that Vladek so cleverly wields during their imprisonment, yet she manages to survive. After the war, they move to Stockholm, where Art is born. She persuades Vladek to move to New York so she can be closer to her surviving relatives. When her nephew Lolek is killed in a car accident, her depression spirals out of control. She never recovers and commits suicide four years later in 1968. Anja's suicide is the subject of Art's comic-within-a-comic, "Prisoner on the Hell Planet," in which he blames his dead mother for the perfect crime of psychologically murdering him. He depicts her as a needy woman, asking her son, who has just been discharged from a mental hospital, if he still loves her.

Art Spiegelman

Art Spiegelman is the autobiographer of *Maus*. He is Vladek and Anja's son, a comic book writer intent on publishing his father's Holocaust story as a graphic novel. At times he portrays himself in a negative light. In "Prisoner on the Hell Planet," he blames his mother for murdering him as a result of her suicide, and at the end of Volume I he calls his father a murderer for having burned his mother's diaries about the war.

Like his mother, Art has suffered from mental illness, having checked himself into a mental hospital at age twenty following a nervous breakdown. At the time of the story, he is happily married, and at the beginning of Volume II, he and Françoise are expecting a child.

Art struggles with survivor's guilt, even though he was born after the Holocaust. In the beginning of Volume II, this guilt manifests itself as writer's block. He is bothered by the fact that life has been much easier for him than for his parents. Even worse, he has had an ongoing sibling rivalry with the photograph of his dead brother, which hangs in his parents' bedroom.

Art presents himself as an honest autobiographer and biographer. He could easily have drawn himself in a flattering way, but he does not. He includes stories his father has told him to omit, such as his affair with a woman before he met Anja. Art is conflicted about his father; he admires Vladek for his perseverance during the war, but he loathes the miserly, racist old man he has become.

Art is overwhelmed by the success of the first volume of *Maus* and shrinks—literally—from the media attention he receives. He works through his conflicted feelings about survivor's guilt and writer's block with his therapist but presents himself as a person wearing a mouse mask rather than as having a real mouse head during their session. In fact, Art suggests that the true survivor of *Maus: A Survivor's Tale* is himself, not Vladek. The last frame of Volume II gives Vladek's death year as 1982, years before the first volume was published, and the last name on the page—underneath Vladek and Anja's tombstone—is Art's.

Mala Spiegelman

Mala Spiegelman is a Holocaust survivor and Vladek's second wife. She knew Vladek and Anja before the war in Poland. Her parents were killed when the Sosnowiec Jews gathered at the sports stadium and then were sent to the camps. She marries Vladek following Anja's suicide and wonders how Anja put up with him for so many years. She complains endlessly about Vladek's miserly ways, insisting that she does not have enough money to buy herself essential items. Other Holocaust survivors are not nearly as stingy, she believes. She frequently threatens to leave him and ultimately does, taking much of his money with her. She is highstrung and calls upon Art for assistance in dealing with Vladek, especially after they reunite in Florida and he has yet another heart attack. She thinks Vladek values things more than people.

Richieu Spiegelman

Richieu is Anja and Vladek's first son, born in 1937. After the war begins, his parents send him away, presumably to a safer place. Instead, his Aunt Tosha poisons him, along with herself and her own two children, because she fears they are about to be sent to a concentration camp. Volume II is dedicated to Richieu, whose photograph appears on the dedication page. Art states that he endured a sibling rivalry with Richieu's photograph for his entire childhood. Art got into all sorts of trouble, but Richieu's photograph never did. At the end of the second volume, Vladek, ill and confused, calls Art Richieu by mistake, a Freudian slip that may indicate that the dead son is never far from the father's thoughts.

Vladek Spiegelman

Vladek Spiegelman is the story's main character. He relates his experiences before and during World War II to his son, Art, during a series of conversations during the late 1970s and early 1980s. Vladek is a survivor of Auschwitz, a notorious Nazi concentration camp in Poland where millions of Jews were killed as part of Adolf Hitler's Final Solution. As a young man, Vladek is successful in business and marries Anja, the daughter of a wealthy man. When the war starts,

Vladek's knack for making deals to ensure his survival becomes obvious. He finds his way back home after becoming a prisoner of war, and as food is rationed and Jews are restricted from many daily activities, Vladek finds ways to do business to feed his family.

When Jews are being rounded up and sent to Auschwitz, Vladek hides his family in a cellar and then in an attic. After the ghetto is liquidated, he keeps himself and Anja safe for quite a while by arranging to hide in a townhouse and a barn. He always finds food, pays others for protection, and never takes advantage of people unfairly. He is honest, faithful, cautious, and knows whom to trust. He has the will to survive when Anja does not, and he urges her to work hard to stay alive.

As an old man in failing health at the time he tells his story to Art, however, Vladek is manipulative, miserly, and racist. He throws his son's coat away because he does not like it, returns opened boxes of food to the grocery store, reuses tea bags, and calls an African American man a *shvartser*, a derogative Yiddish term. He complains that his second wife wants to steal his money, he sneaks into the swimming pool of a Catskills hotel, and he feigns a heart attack to get his son to visit him.

Other people's misery does not register with Vladek. Mala is infuriated by his attachment to things instead of people, but he thinks she is only after his money. He believes that when he and Anja were reunited after the war, they lived happily ever after, but twenty years later Anja commits suicide and his son has a nervous breakdown. Vladek is tormented over the suicide of his beloved Anja, but he never expresses regret over failing to do something about her misery. He burns her diaries of the war after her death because of the painful memories they harbor.

In Auschwitz, Vladek's bravery reaches new heights. He capitalizes on his English language skills to win favor from the kapo. He routinely risks his life to smuggle food to Anja and talk to her occasionally. He volunteers for work for which he is not qualified, knowing he can pick up valuable new skills quickly. He never passes up an opportunity to barter his skills for food. He is a faithful friend who arranges to get Mandelbaum a belt and shoes that fit.

After the prisoners are marched out of Auschwitz, Vladek's survival skills reach their zenith. He ties a blanket to the ceiling of a cattle car to suspend himself above the mass of dying prisoners and becomes one of a handful of survivors because he can reach the snow on the roof. Later, felled by typhus, he pays others to take him to the bathroom. Even with one foot in the grave, he finds a way to barter for what he needs to save his life. When he can no longer eat, he gives them his food, and in return they help him leave Dachau rather than let him die in the abandoned camp.

Despite his inconsiderateness, Vladek appreciates Art very much, supports his work on the book, and shares his story as a way to spend time with him. However, at the end of his story, Vladek, in a weakened state, mistakenly calls Art "Richieu," indicating that he has never forgotten the dead boy and may feel closer in spirit to him than to his living son.

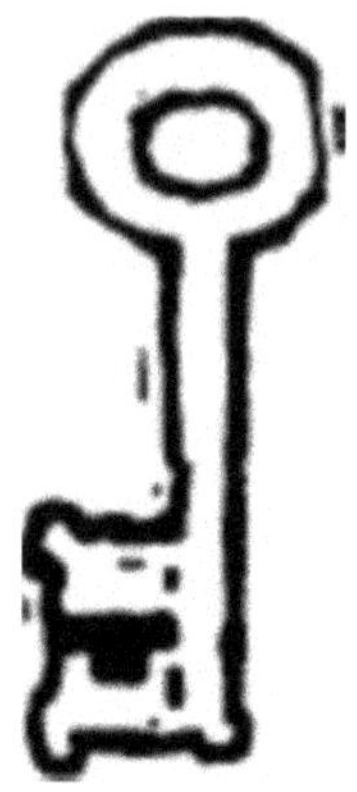

Topics for Further Study

- Marjane Satrapi's *Persepolis* is a graphic novel for young adults published in two volumes like *Maus*. It is the autobiography of a privileged young girl growing up in Tehran during the Islamic Revolution who eventually immigrates to Vienna to escape oppression. Though the circumstances are different, Satrapi experiences hardships similar to those suffered by Vladek and Anja in World War II Poland. Write an essay describing the similarities between the plights of the Satrapis and the Spiegelmans.

- Make a chart to document instances in which Spiegelman draws something in the frame yet does not comment on it in the text. For each example, explain what the unremarked visual item adds to the story.

- Spiegelman illustrated *Maus* in a much different style than "Prisoner on the Hell Planet." In an essay, explain why you think he did this and how both illustration styles impact their respective stories.

- Research post-traumatic stress disorder (PTSD) online and find out what its common symptoms are. Create a short class presentation about PTSD or invite a healthcare professional to discuss the topic. Then divide the class into three groups to debate whether Anja, Vladek, and Art suffer from PTSD and why. Have each group present their findings to the class.

- Visit a local Holocaust museum or read a nonfiction account of World War II (such as Primo Levi's *Survival in Auschwitz* or *The Diary of Anne Frank*, a favorite of teenage readers. Create a Wikispace about how Vladek's experiences compare to other accounts of life in the Jewish ghettos and the concentration camps. Invite others to post information on your space, including Holocaust survivors and their relatives who may be able to add information.

Themes

Survival

The theme of survival is evident from the book's subtitle: *A Survivor's Tale*. While Vladek is the most obvious survivor of *Maus*, he is not the only one. Anja, who also lived through the Holocaust, survived for a number of years before the psychological toll of events prompts her suicide. Art is a survivor too, as evidenced by his signature on the last page of the story beneath the drawing of his parents' gravestone. In fact, many critics have noted that it is Art, not Vladek, who is the survivor of the title. This is suggested by the frame story, in which Art autobiographically depicts himself as surviving Vladek's exasperating antics and prevailing in his decades-long quest to bring his father's story to light.

A corollary of survival—survivor's guilt—looms large in the story. Art's guilt over his mother's death is melded with his anxieties about the Holocaust most vividly in "Prisoner on the Hell Planet," which shows him wearing a prison inmate's outfit (indistinguishable from a concentration camp uniform) and incarcerated for his mother's perfect crime—injecting him with a lethal dose of guilt through her suicide. Art also discusses survivor's guilt with Françoise and his therapist, Pavel. He feels guilty for having survived while his brother died and for having a much easier life than his parents. Finally, Volume II of *Maus* is dedicated to Richieu, who did not survive, and Nadja Spiegelman, his recently born niece who will usher in a new generation of the surviving Spiegelman family.

Family Relationships

The frame story of *Maus* depicts the relationship between Art and Vladek Spiegelman in Vladek's later years. It starts with Art's first visit to his father's home in two years. Their strained relationship is put aside when Art persuades Vladek to tell his story of the Holocaust. These occasions become an opportunity for them to spend time together. Vladek enjoys having Art around, but Art is more interested in writing his book than enjoying Vladek's company. Art continually deflects Vladek's concerns about his troubled relationship with Mala, money, home improvement, and his failing health.

While Art and Vladek's relationship is central to the story, Anja's relationship to Art is also important. Art becomes interested in Anja's Holocaust story only when he begins his book, even though her diaries had been around until after her death. Just before her suicide, Anja asks Art if he loves her, and he begrudgingly says he does. He reacts violently to Anja's suicide and Vladek's grief, believing himself to be the victim of the neediness of both parents. When he finds out his father has burned Anja's diaries, Art calls Vladek a murderer, echoing his words following his mother's suicide. The Spiegelman family seems dysfunctional for not being able to acknowledge one another's pain. Vladek, for his part, believes that he and Anja lived happily ever after following the war, oblivious to the fact that she was miserable enough to commit suicide. In his second marriage, Mala and Vladek argue continually, neither one obtaining any degree of compassion or insight into the feelings of the other. After Mala leaves him, Art and Françoise (who appear to have a very healthy relationship) reject the idea of taking care of Vladek themselves. During the Holocaust, Vladek went to great, if futile, lengths to keep Anja's family safe, and now Art tries desperately to avoid having to do the same for Vladek.

Suffering

Closely related to the theme of family relationships is the theme of suffering. There are two types of suffering depicted in *Maus*. The first is the suffering of Vladek, Anja, and their families during World War II, when they were imprisoned, forced to hide, suffer starvation and illness, or killed outright. The second type of suffering happens after the Holocaust and concerns not only Vladek and Anja, but also Art and Mala. Vladek screams in his sleep—a situation the youthful Art believes is normal, and Anja suffers depression that leads to suicide. These lingering effects of the Holocaust cause Art to suffer guilt over having a better life than his parents.

Art and Mala both suffer from Vladek's extreme stinginess and constant complaining. The story-within-the-story, "Prisoner on the Hell Planet," depicts Art's mental anguish in the wake of his nervous breakdown—more suffering, albeit without much explanation. In Volume II, Art explains his creative and existential suffering in the chapter "Auschwitz (Time Flies)," in which he wonders if the world needs to hear another Holocaust story and how he should tell such a story, and by illustrating his ambivalence over the success of the book's first volume by drawing himself rising above a pile of dead bodies.

Creative Process

The main theme of the frame story in *Maus* is the creative process. Art draws himself recording Vladek's story, laboring over the creation of *Maus*, and suffering from conflicting feelings about the work's success. The second volume opens with Art and Françoise discussing which animal she should be drawn as—her French nationality and conversion to Judaism presenting a predicament. The chapter "Auschwitz (Time Flies)" is key to the theme of the creative process. Art draws himself in his studio, suffering from depression and writer's block in the wake of the first volume's publication. Barbed wire is visible outside the window, along with a prison-like spotlight. Dead bodies pile up at his feet. He is trapped by history, imprisoned by his inability to render the rest of Vladek's story.

The second half of the sequence shows Art at his therapist's office. Their conversation about Art's writer's block touches on guilt and whether or not there should be more Holocaust stories. The scene ends comically with Art quoting Samuel Beckett on the meaninglessness of speech. Pavel, the therapist, comments that he should put that quote in his book. The creative process theme is also evident in the dates Spiegelman ascribes to himself at the end next to his signature beneath his parents' grave: 1978–1991. These are not his birth and death years but rather the years in which he labored over writing the book.

Style

Frame Narrative

Maus is written in the form of a story-within-a story. The story of Art and Vladek is the frame narrative that surrounds the Holocaust story of Vladek and Anja. The Holocaust narrative is told in flashback form, which allows Vladek to share his eyewitness account in Spiegelman's autobiography. Art plays the role of historian, coaxing details from Vladek and providing the central metaphor of Jews as mice and Germans as cats. Art is a witness to Vladek's story, rarely questioning his account (except for the part about the orchestra at Auschwitz), serves as a surrogate for the reader in reacting to the horrors Vladek describes, and provides visual details of Vladek's story through his drawings. By providing this frame story, Spiegelman gives additional context to the Holocaust, especially in terms of its lingering effects on survivors and the children of survivors.

The frame technique contrasts the difference between Vladek as a young man—smart, resourceful, willful, and deliberate—with his older self—miserly, manipulative, and racist. For example, in Auschwitz Vladek saves the paper wrapping from the kapo's cheese, on which he writes a note to Anja. While he relates his story to Art, he picks up a scrap of wire from the sidewalk, claiming it has many uses. The first action is resourceful, the second is obsessive (Vladek has plenty of money should he need to buy wire), but as the frame narrative makes clear, the only difference between the two instances is Vladek's circumstances. Spiegelman relates these events in his quest to uncover Vladek's true nature—maybe he was just as difficult during the war as he was afterward, but in one situation his resourcefulness saved his life and in another it represents an unhealthy attachment to things instead of people.

The story of Anja's suicide and its impact on Art is told within the frame narrative as well, through the inclusion of Spiegelman's "Prisoner on the Hell Planet: A Case History" comic, first published in *Short Order Comix* in 1972, an underground magazine that Spiegelman coedited. Its inclusion is jarring because of the stark woodcut-style artwork that renders Art and his mother as people instead of mice.

Autobiography

Maus was initially considered fiction—it even charted on the *New York Times* fiction bestseller list until Spiegelman persuaded them to move it to nonfiction. Despite the fact that the characters are rendered as animals, *Maus* is Art Spiegelman's autobiography of the period in his life where he seeks out his father's story and tries to make sense of it. Embedded in Art's autobiography is Vladek's autobiography; the frame narrative becomes a savvy way to provide a maximum amount of story in a minimum amount of space. Underscoring the autobiographical nature of both their stories is the inclusion of several photographs. The photograph of Richieu (on the dedication page for Volume II), the 1958 vacation snapshot of Art and Anja at the beginning of “Prisoner on the Hell Planet,” and the studio portrait of Vladek wearing a concentration camp uniform after the war reveal the human beings behind the text's generic mouse drawings.

Maus is a specific type of autobiography—a Kunstlerroman, literally an artist's novel (from the German word for artist, *kunstler*). A Kunstlerroman portrays the writer as he or she embarks on a journey to artistic maturity. Notable Kunstlerromans in literary history include Thomas Mann's *Death in Venice*, James Joyce's *Portrait of the Artist as a Young Man*, and Virginia Woolf's *To the Lighthouse*. The writer of a Kunstlerroman is often a sensitive youth who rejects the bourgeois (middle-class) notions of his or her upbringing. While Spiegelman was not necessarily young when he wrote *Maus*, he was sensitive. His precarious mental state is depicted in “Prisoner on the Hell Planet” and in the portions of the frame narrative that deal with his guilt, depression, and anger. The dates next to his signature at the book's end, 1978–1991, encapsulate the years of his artistic journey and signal that the journey has come to an end.

Metaphor

The metaphor of *Maus* is evident from the book's title, which was inspired by Adolf Hitler's assertion that Jews were an inferior race who bred like vermin, thus giving him the moral right to exterminate them. In drawing Polish Jews as mice, Spiegelman underscores how the Nazi Party dehumanized an entire race of people, and in showing Germans as cats he signals their power over the Jews. Spiegelman continues the metaphor with other nationalities: the Polish gentiles are pigs; the Americans are dogs; and the French are frogs. This visual symbolism underscores that fact that one cause of the Holocaust was the inability to see past people's nationality and ethnicity and evaluate them as individuals. Completing Spiegelman's mouse metaphor is the fact that the gas used by the Nazis to exterminate the Jews—the Zyklon B brand of hydrogen cyanide—had been previously used to kill cockroaches.

Using animals as stand-ins for people has an illustrious literary history. From Aesop's Fables to Franz Kafka's "Josephine the Singer, or the Mouse Folk" to George Orwell's *Animal Farm* and E. B. White's *Charlotte's Web*, generations of writers have anthropomorphized animals in the interest of storytelling. In comics the tradition is even stronger. George Herriman's *Krazy Kat*, originated in 1913, included a cat, a mouse, and a dog. Walt Disney debuted Mickey Mouse in 1928 and added numerous animal pals to the gang in subsequent years; Walt Kelley's *Pogo* and Charles Schulz's *Peanuts* are two more recent examples.

Graphic Novel

A graphic novel is a book-length story told through a combination of words and images arranged in panel format. As a literary form, it has a short history. Will Eisner's *A Contract with God*, published in 1978, is considered by many to be the birth of the genre. The mainstream success of the first volume of *Maus* just eight years later opened the door for many other graphic novelists.

The main unit of the graphic novel is the page. Within a page the artist draws panels that can be edited to a certain degree, similar to a scenes in a film, but once a page is designed it is difficult to rework it without impacting other pages as well. Whereas many novelists might think in terms of chapters, graphic novelists think in terms of the number of panels on a page and how to economize both words and images in order to capture only the details necessary to tell the story.

The advantage of *Maus* over other Holocaust memoirs is its visual narrative. Spiegelman illustrates Vladek's stories with drawings and diagrams of hiding places and the Auschwitz gas chambers and maps of Auschwitz and Birkenau. In Vladek's story of how he learned to be a shoemaker, Spiegelman draws a diagram of how his father sewed an officer's leather boots together, thereby securing himself extra food. In these instances, a picture really is worth a thousand words. Another advantage of graphic novels is the author's ability to draw one thing and say another or to have the image and the text subtly askew. This succinct dissonance adds richness to the story. For example, when Vladek, Art, and Françoise are driving to the grocery store, Vladek tells of four girls in Auschwitz who tried to revolt and were hanged. Rather than depict the girls in a flashback, Spiegelman draws himself, Vladek, and Françoise meandering through the Catskills on the way to the grocery store. The bare feet of the four hanged girls hover in the foreground of the frame.

Combining both stories into a single image exemplifies the narrative economy of a graphic novel. It also suggests that the ghosts of the Holocaust's six million victims live in the memories of the survivors, half a world away from where the horror took place.

Historical Context

The Jewish Ghetto

The details of Vladek's story are historically accurate. Beginning in 1939, the Germans quarantined Poland's Jews into small, tightly packed ghettos. They lacked sufficient food, clothing, and other amenities. As the war continued, the ghettos became de facto concentration camps. Of the Polish ghettos, Warsaw's was the largest, with three hundred eighty thousand residents—30 percent of the city's population—living on 2.4 percent of its land. The ghetto was walled off, and those who attempted to escape were shot. Conditions were such that many died of disease and starvation. By 1944, many ghettos were liquidated, meaning everyone was killed or sent to concentration camps.

Sosnowiec, Poland, where Vladek and Anja lived, had roughly thirty thousand Jewish residents at the start of World War II. Because of its location on the German-Polish border, it was one of the first cities to be occupied by the Germans and one of the first to suffer wide-scale executions. During the early years of the war, the Jewish residents were used as slave laborers for the German war effort. In late 1942, just as Vladek describes, the remaining residents of the ghetto were moved to nearby Srodula or taken to Auschwitz. The ghetto was liquidated in the spring of 1944. Today, Sosnowiec is a thriving metropolis of two million people, but the number of Jewish citizens is unknown. Roughly twenty thousand Jews lived in all of Poland in 2006.

Auschwitz

The Final Solution was the Nazi Party's plan for carrying out systematic genocide against European Jews. The plan called for the construction of several extermination camps inside Poland to make the slaughter organized and efficient. Once the Jews were rounded up in the ghettos, they were transported to the camps via existing railroads. They were divided into two groups upon arrival, with one group sent immediately to the gas chambers and the other to barracks in order to provide slave labor until they were killed. Dead bodies were incinerated in crematoria or buried in pits. Auschwitz I opened in 1940 and was initially a work camp. As the Holocaust intensified, the camp was expanded. Birkenau (Auschwitz II) became operational in 1942, and a majority of the more than one million people who died in Auschwitz were killed in its gas chambers. As Spiegelman states in the chapter "Auschwitz (Time Flies)," the Hungarian Jews were killed at an unprecedented rate in the spring of 1944—over four hundred thousand in less than three months.

Compare & Contrast

- **1940s:** Suffering from depression,

Anja Spiegelman visits a sanitarium near the Czechoslovakian border—possibly in Gorbersdorf, a resort town that attracts wealthy visitors from all over Europe.
1970s: Art Spiegelman suffers a nervous breakdown and is admitted to a state mental institution, a common treatment of the day, where he stays for several weeks. A nervous breakdown indicates a person is unable to function in everyday life because of anxiety and depression, although it is not a medical diagnosis.
Today: In-patient treatment for mental illness is rare, as most state mental institutions have shut their doors. Treatment commonly consists of medication dispensed through out-patient clinics.

- **1940s:** The Nazis kill six million people during World War II. Jews, Polish gentiles, Soviet prisoners, homosexuals, Roma, and mentally and physically handicapped people are all targeted.
  1970s: Pol Pot, the leader of the Khmer Rouge and the de facto ruler of Cambodia, orders the deaths of two hundred thousand people, mostly Chinese, between 1975 and 1979. In total, 1.5 to 2.5 million

people die from disease, starvation, oppression, and violence. Many historians consider it the worst genocide of the Cold War era.

Today: Since 2003, the war in Darfur, Sudan, has displaced up to two million people and caused the deaths of three hundred thousand more people. Though some believe the conflict is a genocide, others disagree, stating that the intent to abolish an entire race is not present.

- **1940s:** Wealthy Jewish tourists visit European spa towns such as Czechoslovakia's Karolvy Vary, the site of a renowned mineral hot springs, resort hotels, and sanitariums, some of which allow Jewish guests.

  1970s: Jewish families living in New York frequent the many resorts run by and for Jewish people in the Catskill Mountains, but with many postwar immigrants nearing retirement, Florida gains in popularity as a vacation destination.

  Today: Jewish travelers can enjoy a variety of kosher tours worldwide, and young adults are encouraged to visit Israel through nonprofit organizations that sponsor free vacations as part of their birthright.

The Auschwitz death march Vladek endured began on January 17, 1945. Sixty thousand prisoners were evacuated to the Gross-Rosen concentration camp about one hundred miles away. Tens of thousands died along the way, either during the march itself or in overcrowded cattle cars as they were transported to their final destination. The seventy-five hundred remaining Auschwitz prisoners—those too weak to march—were liberated by the Soviet Army on January 27, 1945. In total about three hundred thousand former Auschwitz prisoners survived the war. In 1947, Auschwitz became amuseum, and since then millions of visitors have walked beneath the infamous Arbeit Macht Frei ("Work Brings Freedom") sign emblazoned over its gates, which Spiegelman reproduces in the first volume of *Maus*.

Holocaust Survivors in New York

From 1945 to 1952, between eighty thousand and one hundred forty thousand Holocaust survivors immigrated to the United States from the displaced persons camps in Europe. About half settled in the New York area, and many others moved to southern Florida. Rego Park, a neighborhood in Queens, a borough of New York City, welcomed a number of these immigrants with amenities that included existing synagogues, affordable housing, and plentiful business opportunities. Over the years, many of these Jews have moved away, and more recent Soviet Jewish immigrants have taken their place.

During the humid New York City summer, many Jews vacationed in the Catskill Mountains northwest of the city. Family-run resorts catered to a Jewish clientele and fostered an atmosphere of community. Jewish comedians played in the resorts' lounges, a circuit that came to be known as the Borscht Belt. Children spent the summer in sleep-away camps, and during Jewish holidays the resorts were packed. By the 1970s as Jewish immigrants became more assimilated or retired to Florida, the resorts of the Catskills fell into decline. However, many older New Yorkers, such as Vladek Spiegelman, continued to vacation there.

The Rise of Independent Comix

In the late 1960s and early 1970s, Spiegelman was an influential figure in the rise of underground comics, or comix, as they were often called. Writers such as Spiegelman, Robert Crumb, and Bill Griffith self-published often graphic and profane autobiographical stories infused with large doses of self-loathing, violence, sex, and cultural criticism. The scene thrived in San Francisco, where Robert Crumb published *Zap* and Bill Griffith and Spiegelman edited *Short Order Comix*, an anthology devoted to stories of no more than four pages. Issue Number 1 in 1973 included "Prisoner on the Hell Planet." By the time Spiegelman returned to New York and launched *RAW* (in which *Maus* was initially serialized) with Mouly in 1980, the underground scene was morphing into an independent scene that paved the way for the alternative comics of the late 1980s and 1990s.

Critical Overview

Maus was published to overwhelming critical acclaim. When the first volume appeared in 1986, graphic novels were unfamiliar to many readers. The success of the first volume fostered acceptance of the genre and paved the way for other graphic novelists, including Joe Sacco, Chris Ware, and Marjane Satrapi. As a Holocaust narrative, the book was lauded as well. In a *New York Times Book Review* assessment of *And Here My Troubles Began*, Lawrence L. Langer comments that "perhaps no Holocaust narrative will ever contain the whole experience. But Art Spiegelman has found an original and authentic form to draw us closer to its bleak heart." Writing in *VLS*, Laurie Muchnick applauds Spiegelman for creating "the perfect structure: *Maus* 's horror is intimate yet tolerable, its presentation gimmicky but expressive." In his review for *Newsweek*, David Gates admires "the comforting artificiality of an animal cartoon [that] worked both as savage irony and as a nearly transparent surface through which human horror could be imagined."

A few critics question Spiegelman's use of animals to represent ethnicity and nationality, claiming it perpetuates stereotypes. In an essay for *Commentary*, Hillel Halkin states that it is wrong to believe that Germans killed Jews and the Poles allowed it to happen because "cats kill mice, who do not attack cats, while pigs do not care about either." Instead, Halkin maintains, "the Holocaust was a crime committed by humans against humans, not—as Nazi theory held—by one biological species against another." Others think that Spiegelman did not take full advantage of the graphics portion of a graphic novel and that his drawings are mere illustrations rather than a vital component of the narrative. James Walton, who generally praises *And Here My Troubles Began*, writes in *Spectator* that by the time Vladek reaches Auschwitz, Spiegelman has run out of sufficient tools with which to tell the story. "The most horrifying set pieces, the living and dead being burned together in mass graves … simply don't work as cartoons," Walton writes. "They seem both melodramatic and bathetic, inadequate images of his father's words."

In the years since the book's publication, many scholars have sought to assess *Maus* 's place within the body of Holocaust literature. Michael E. Staub, writing in *MELUS*, notes that *Maus* is "very much about … the tensions involved in understanding what it means to have a Jewish identity in a post-Auschwitz age."

Maus "has been embraced by both popular and academic readers," writes Joshua L. Charlson in *Arizona Quarterly*. Charlson admires how Spiegelman uses the "trivialized" art form of the comic strip, populated with anthropomorphic animals, as a "profound meditation on the historical event considered by many the gravest in its ethical implications for the twentieth century."

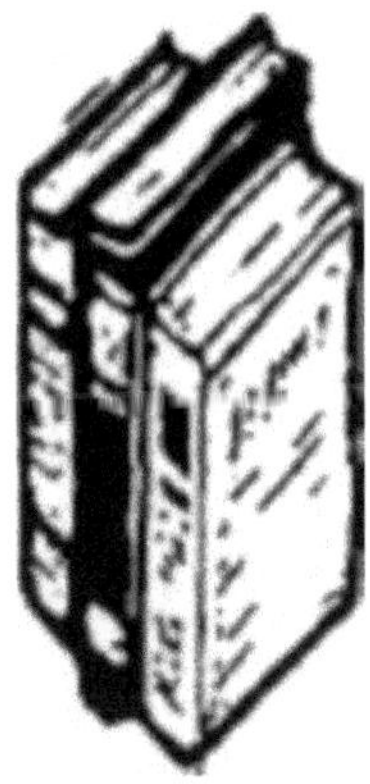

What Do I Read Next?

- Art Spiegelman's *In the Shadow of No Towers* (2004) is the author's account of 9/11, which he witnessed firsthand from his home in lower Manhattan. The collection of comics documents his struggle to come to terms with terrorism, Islamic fundamentalism, and the U.S. government's subsequent war on terror.
- Anne Frank began *The Diary of a Young Girl* on her twelfth birthday, and it chronicles the two years she and her family hid from the Nazis in occupied Amsterdam. Eventually discovered, Frank died in Bergen-Belsen concentration camp shortly before the end of the war. Her

manuscript was first published in the United States in 1952 and has since been adapted for stage and film. The Frank family's experiences bear many similarities to those of Vladek and Anja as they sought to avoid being sent to the camps.

- As a teenager, Nobel Peace Prize laureate Elie Wiesel was imprisoned in Auschwitz and survived the death march to Buchenwald. His short memoir *Night* documents his plight, during which he ignores his father's dying words and explores his loss of faith in religion and humankind. Originally written in Yiddish and first published in 1955, the book met with indifference when published in the United States in 1960. It has since sold millions of copies and become the first volume of a trilogy that includes the novels *Dawn* (1961) and *Day* (also known as *The Accident*) (1962).
- Chris Ware's graphic novel *Jimmy Corrigan, the Smartest Kid on Earth* (2000) won an American Book Award in 2001. The story, first serialized in Ware's periodic *Acme Novelty Library*, is told partly in flashback form and concerns the relationship of an isolated, middle-

aged man with his overbearing mother and his estranged father, whom he has met only once.

- Marjane Satrapi's *Persepolis: Story of a Childhood* (2003) and *Persepolis 2: Story of a Return* (2004) are autobiographical graphic novels about Satrapi's youth in Iran during the Islamic Revolution, a time of violence and social upheaval. Fearing for Marjane's safety, her parents send her to school in Vienna, where she finds life as an expatriate teenager difficult. Succumbing to homesickness, she returns to Iran and finds it a much different place than she remembers.
- Joe Sacco won the American Book Award in 1996 for his two-volume graphic novel *Palestine*, a journalistic account of his travels to the West Bank and Gaza Strip in 1991 to document everyday life in the occupied territories during the long-standing violent confrontation between the Palestinians and the Israelis.
- Scott McCloud's award-winning *Understanding Comics: The Invisible Art* (1993) is a comic book that introduces readers to the genre of comic books and graphic novels.

McCloud traces the history of the medium and provides insight on specific advantages of the form.

- Gilbert Hernandez's *Palomar: The Heartbreak Soup Stories* (2003) is a graphic novel that collects thirteen years' worth of Hernandez's stories about the interconnected lives of residents in the small Central American town of Palomar. The stories embody the complex family histories and emotional lives of their characters in a concise, spare style that sometimes employs the kind of magic realism common in Latin American literature.

Sources

Berkwits, Jeff, "What's with Jewish Comedy?," in *San Diego Jewish Journal*, August 2004.

Charlson, Joshua L., "Framing the Past: Postmodernism and the Making of Reflective Memory in Art Spiegelman's *Maus*," in *Arizona Quarterly*, Vol. 57, No. 3, Autumn 2001, pp. 91–120.

"The Extermination of the Jews of Sosnowiec, Bendzin, and Vicinity," in *Holocaust Education and Archive Research Team (H.E.A.R.T.)*, http://www.holocaustresearchproject.org/nazioccupa (accessed December 9, 2009).

Gass, William H., "Philosophy and the Form of Fiction," in *Fiction and the Figures of Life: Essays*, Knopf, 1970, pp. 3–26.

Gates, David, "Stories Out of the Silence," in *Newsweek*, Vol. 119, No. 4, January 27, 1992, p. 59.

Gopnik, Adam, "High and Low: Modern Art and Popular Culture," in *New York Museum of Modern Art* exhibition catalog, 1991, pp. 153–229.

Groth, Gary, "An Interview with Art Spiegelman," in *Comics Journal*, No. 180, September 1995, pp. 52–114.

Halkin, Hillel, "Inhuman Comedy," in *Commentary*, Vol. 93, No. 2, February 1992, pp. 55–56.

Laga, Barry, "*Maus*, Holocaust, and History: Redrawing the Frame," in *Arizona Quarterly*, Vol. 57, No. 1, Spring 2001, pp. 61–90.

Langer, Lawrence L., "A Fable of the Holocaust," in *New York Times Book Review*, November 3, 1991, pp. 1, 35–36.

Muchnick, Laurie, Review of *Maus* in *VLS*, No. 101, December 1991, p. 16.

Spiegelman, Art, *Maus: A Survivor's Tale*, Volume I: *My Father Bleeds History*, Pantheon, 1986.

Spiegelman, Art, *Maus: A Survivor's Tale*, Volume II: *And Here My Troubles Began*, Pantheon, 1991.

Staub, Michael E., "The Shoah Goes On and On: Remembrance and Representation in Art Spiegelman's *Maus*," in *MELUS*, Vol. 20, No. 3, Fall 1995, pp. 33–46.

Walton, James, "Nothing Comic about the Holocaust," in *Spectator*, Vol. 268, No. 8543, April 4, 1992, p. 33.

Young, James E., "Thc Holocaust as Vicarious Past: Art Spiegelman's *Maus* and the Afterimages of History," in *Critical Inquiry*, Vol. 24, No. 3, Spring 1998, pp. 666–99.

Further Reading

Cohen, Beth B., *Case Closed: Holocaust Survivors in Postwar America*, Rutgers University Press, 2007.

> Cohen is a psychologist and social historian who examines primary documents in her quest to understand the difficulties that Jewish displaced persons—especially orphans and Orthodox Jews—had in adjusting to American life in New York and other locations.

Doherty, Thomas, "Art Spiegelman's *Maus*: Graphic Art and the Holocaust," in *American Literature*, Vol. 68, 1996, pp. 69–84.

> Doherty analyzes the power of Spiegelman's illustrations in terms of how they replicate cinematic conventions and compare with the Third Reich's predilection for idealized human forms in their own films.

Epstein, Helen, *Children of the Holocaust: Conversations with Sons and Daughters of Survivors*, Penguin, 1988.

> Epstein is the daughter of Holocaust survivors and examines the precarious mental balancing act it

entailed, especially in childhood. She examines the history of Holocaust survivors as they made their way to South America and New York and discusses the idea of survivor syndrome at length.

Gass, William H., "Philosophy and the Form of Fiction," in *Fiction and the Figures of Life: Essays*, Knopf, 1970.

Gass coins the term "breaking the fourth wall" in this essay, although he does not discuss the concept at length. The essay is deeply philosophical.

Geis, Deborah R., ed., *Considering Maus: Approaches to Art Spiegelman's "Survivor's Tale" of the Holocaust*, revised ed., University of Alabama Press, 2007.

This collection of essays by prominent scholars offers numerous interpretations and insight into Spiegelman's opus, including its impact on popular culture, its graphic arts influences, its relationship to psychoanalysis, and its success as a work of oral history.

Hatfield, Charles, "Irony and Self-Reflexivity in Autobiographical Comics: Two Case Studies," in *Alternative Comics: An Emerging Literature*, University Press of Mississippi, 2005, pp. 128–51.

Hatfield considers *Maus* at length (as well as Justin Green's *Binky Brown Meets the Holy Virgin Mary*) and praises it for its complexity and how it tackles a topic that the author himself considers unpresentable.

"Holocaust Encyclopedia," in *United States Holocaust Memorial Museum*, http://www.ushmm.org.

The United States Holocaust Museum's online encyclopedia presents photographs and data regarding many aspects of the Holocaust, including statistics regarding the Polish ghettos, the pogroms, and concentration camps.

Witek, Joseph, ed., *Art Spiegelman: Conversations*, University Press of Mississippi, 2007.

A volume in the "Conversations with Comic Artists" series, this volume collects interviews with Spiegelman from 1976 to 2006, including some never before published. Spiegelman discusses all aspects of his career, including *Maus* and *In the Shadow of No Towers*.

Suggested Search Terms

Art Spiegelman

children of Holocaust survivors

Holocaust AND graphic novel

Maus AND survivor's guilt

graphic novel AND autobiography

Auschwitz AND Spiegelman

Maus AND Spiegelman

graphic novel AND Spiegelman

Complete Maus AND Spiegelman

themes AND Spiegelman

Lightning Source UK Ltd.
Milton Keynes UK
UKHW020233160819
348040UK00010B/1689/P